Dee Johnson

SPELLS
for
SELF-CARE

First published in Great Britain in 2024 by

Greenfinch
An imprint of Quercus Editions Ltd
Carmelite House
50 Victoria Embankment
London EC4Y 0DZ

An Hachette UK company

Copyright © 2024 Dee Johnson

The moral right of Dee Johnson to be identified as the author of this work has been asserted in accordance with the Copyright, Designs and Patents Act, 1988.

All rights reserved. No part of this publication may be reproduced or transmitted in any form or by any means, electronic or mechanical, including photocopy, recording, or any information storage and retrieval system, without permission in writing from the publisher.

A CIP catalogue record for this book is available from the British Library

HB ISBN 978-1-52943-901-4
Ebook ISBN 978-1-52943-902-1

Quercus Editions Ltd hereby exclude all liability to the extent permitted by law for any errors or omissions in this book and for any loss, damage or expense (whether direct or indirect) suffered by a third party relying on any information contained in this book.

10 9 8 7 6 5 4 3 2 1

Design by Sooky Choi
Cover design and illustrations by Holly Ovenden

Printed and bound in Great Britain by Clays Ltd, Elcograf S.p.A.

MIX
Paper | Supporting responsible forestry
FSC® C104740

Papers used by Greenfinch are from well-managed forests and other responsible sources.

Dee Johnson

SPELLS *for* SELF-CARE

Enchantments for Calm, Relaxation and Joy

greenfinch

CONTENTS

INTRODUCTION..6

THE SPELLS..15
1. MOONSTONE CRYSTAL SOUL HEALING.............16
2. ROSE QUARTZ HARMONY 18
3. MOON MAGICK 20
4. MAGICKAL WATER BOTTLE 22
5. CANDLELIT SELF-CARE BATH 24
6. GREEN SMOOTHIE DETOX..26
7. PERSONAL POWER..28
8. REJUVENATE ME 30
9. BANISH ANXIETY 32
10. SELF-CARE LOVE JAR..34
11. SWEET DREAMS 36
12. GODDESS VENUS INNER BEAUTY 38
13. PROTECTION SPELL 40
14. EMOTIONAL HEALING 42
15. ANTI-DEPRESSION SPELL..44
16. YOUR INNER GODDESS 46
17. YOUR INNER CHILD 48
18. BANISH YOUR WORRIES 50
19. FEEL MORE POWERFUL 52
20. PSYCHIC PROTECTION 54
21. SELF-CONFIDENCE SPELL...56
22. UNCROSSING SPELL...58
23. NEW BEGINNINGS...60
24. GODDESS BATH OIL..62
25. CLEAR MY SKIN 64
26. CLEANSE MY HOME 66

27	CLEANSING AURA SPRAY	68
28	SIMMERING SELF-CARE SOUP	70
29	GOLDEN HOUR MILK	72
30	EMBRACE YOURSELF WITH HAPPINESS	74
31	HEALING MUFFINS	76
32	COMFORTING BEDTIME CACAO	78
33	SPARKLING SELF-CONFIDENCE	80
34	BUTTERFLY MEDITATION	82
35	EMPOWERING SELF-LOVE	84
36	SEVEN CHAKRAS HEALING	86
37	EMBRACE YOUR BEAUTY	88
38	SELF-CARE SPELL FOR ARIES	89
39	INDULGENT BATH RITUAL FOR TAURUS	90
40	RELAXATION SPELL FOR GEMINI	92
41	NOURISHING SPELL FOR CANCER	94
42	SELF-CARE SPELL FOR LEO	96
43	NURTURING SPELL FOR VIRGO	98
44	HARMONIZING SPELL FOR LIBRA	100
45	EMPOWERING SPELL FOR SCORPIO	102
46	BATH RITUAL FOR SAGITTARIUS	104
47	GROUNDING SPELL FOR CAPRICORN	106
48	ENERGY SPELL FOR AQUARIUS	108
49	SELF-CARE SPELL FOR PISCES	109
50	CLEAR YOUR MIND	111

SPELL NOTES	114
INDEX	124
RESOURCES	127
ABOUT THE AUTHOR	128
ACKNOWLEDGEMENTS	128

INTRODUCTION

In today's fast-moving and stressful world, self-care has never been more important. This sweet selection of spells has been created for you to honour and respect your spiritual health and to embark on a healing journey for your emotional well-being. You will find ways to recharge, unwind and manifest. You will discover how to protect your precious life-force energy. And you will learn how to change your habits to make healthy choices using natural ingredients. With mental health issues on the rise in society, finding balance has never been more important. This book allows you to choose a self-care spell that connects with you and supports you.

Self-care spells and rituals lie at the heart of an essential and empowering practice that has gained popularity in recent years. They are cast with the intention of nurturing yourself physically, emotionally and mentally. Incorporating elements of magick and mindfulness, and focusing on intention, these spells have been created to enhance self-love. It is easy to neglect your own needs and prioritize others before yourself. This collection of spells serves as a gentle reminder to think about yourself for a few minutes and to find time in of your busy life to energize and recharge.

These powerful spells encourage you to be better connected to your mind, body and spirit, allowing you to achieve a more harmonious life. From simple spells that use candles and aromatherapy to more elaborate spells with herbs and crystals, each of them can have profound effects on your overall sense of well-being. They can help to reduce stress, to increase self-confidence and will provide a sense of inner peace and tranquillity. Combined with positive, intentional acts, they will help you to take positive steps towards self-love and self-empowerment.

Whether you are entirely new to the world of spell-casting, rituals and magick, or a seasoned practitioner of the arts, the spells in this book offer an accessible way to nurture and connect with yourself on a deeper level. They take you on a magickal journey, empowering you to take charge of our own spiritual well-being and happiness. They are like little acts of magick that help you to restore balance and energy within yourself. Casting a spell can be as simple as lighting a soothing scented candle or taking a rejuvenating bath filled with fragrant herbs and oils. By incorporating these rituals into your daily routines, you can create a sacred space for self-reflection and healing.

Remember, self-care spells are highly personal and unique to each individual. The key is to listen to your intuition and choose practices that resonate with your inner being. Whether it's stargazing under a clear sky or performing a mindful meditation, explore different spells that make you feel connected, grounded and energized. Embrace the magick of self-care spells. Let them be your guiding light in finding inner peace and self-empowerment. With the flicker of candles and the scent of herbs and oils, these enchanting rituals create a sacred, calm space, inviting you to discover the power within you and nurture your essence, while whispering words of magick.

CASTING A SPELL

Casting spells is an art and practice makes perfect. It can be a powerful and enlightening experience. The more spells you cast, the more confident you will feel. Witches believe in the power of spells and use them as a personal means of empowerment. You, too, can have this power. Words and thoughts hold much power – you need to believe in the magick of your spells for them to come true.

Before casting a spell, witches raise their vibration, or energy. This can be done through dance, meditation or by listening to your favourite music. Anything that 'lifts' you is a good choice. . .you are literally charging yourself up to push your spell up and out into the universe. Visualization is popular with witches: visualize a sparkling gold light flowing from the sky and into your head, right down through your body, and flowing out from your feet.

Witches are often naked (skyclad) when working with magick. This is a personal choice. If you prefer, you could wear a special cloak. Be mindful to wrap up warm if you choose to cast your spell outside and it's a cold night. You don't want to be feeling uncomfortable in the middle of your spell-casting – this will be too much of a distraction.

Casting spells requires preparation and a positive approach in order to ignite whichever spell you are performing. Organization is key. When you have worked out the best time to cast your spell, become excited about it. Liken it to a date in your diary, a special night out. This starts to build up energy. Every time you think about the event, you are adding power for a favourable outcome. Consider taking the day off work or cancelling any prior engagements to ensure that you are in a positive mind frame on the day.

Before casting your spell, make sure you will not be interrupted. Turn off your phone, set the scene, light naturally scented candles and dim the lights. Always use a lighter to light candles, and never matches, as the sulphur will kill your spell. Never blow a candle out, but always use a snuffer to extinguish it, otherwise you will blow your spell away.

A ritual bath or shower before casting a spell is important as it cleanses your body of any negative energy you might have picked up during the day. I recommend using a naturally scented bath or shower wash. Your local health food shop will have a good selection.

Spells should come directly from your heart, with positive thoughts only. After a spell has been cast, it's really important not to speak about it as this can weaken or break it. Other people's opinions might not align with yours and negative words from a friend could put doubt into your mind, so it's best to avoid this. Keeping your spell to yourself keeps it pure and strong.

INTENSIFY YOUR POWER

To add extra power to a spell, create an energy ball before casting. Place your hands together, palms cupped and slightly parted. Visualize an electric blue ball between your hands. Shape it into an energy ball of power to assist you in your spell work. When you feel ready, gently push the ball into your solar plexus. This will boost your energy for your spell work.

THE WITCH'S STORE CUPBOARD

The spells in this book are simple and easy to follow – perfect for both a beginner and an advanced practitioner of the arts – and have been created using the following accessible ingredients. Beeswax candles are great if you can source them, otherwise small spell candles are easily found online.

- Cauldron/heatproof dish
- Wand/small branch from a tree
- Coloured spell candles with holders
- Tealights
- Lighter
- Essential oils, including lavender, chamomile, tea tree, jasmine, orange
- Herbs and spices, including lavender, chamomile, jasmine, hibiscus, rose
- Sage smudge sticks
- Incense sticks
- Crystals, including clear quartz, rose quartz, moonstone, amethyst, tiger's eye, black tourmalin
- Tarot cards

THE TIMING OF A SELF-CARE SPELL

Timing is important. As a rule, self-care spells that enhance and heal something within you should be cast on a waxing moon phase – that is, from the new moon to the full moon. Spells banishing something from your life that no longer serves you well should be cast on a waning moon, after the full moon to the dark moon. Take into account how you feel. For example, if you haven't had a great day or are not feeling too well, your energy will be low, so it is best to wait until you're feeling better and uplifted about your spell-casting.

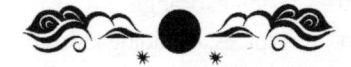

CREATING A SELF-CARE ALTAR

An altar is a great way to enhance your magickal workings as having a permanent space dedicated to love can help amplify your spell-casting. Set one up on a coffee table or a windowsill – or even outside – whatever feels like the right place for you.

- Having found your space, squeeze some lemon juice and mix it with water to cleanse the surface of your altar. A toxin-free cleaner works well, too.

- Add things to make your altar special and unique to you and include candles, moonstone and rose quartz crystals and some lavender.

CAUTION

Never leave candles unattended. Ingredients used in this book are not intended for consumption and should not be consumed for any reason. Be aware of any ingredients you may be sensitive to and patch test on a small area. Do not use if irritation occurs. By going ahead with your spell work, you agree that this book is not responsible for any skin irritation or sensitivity while using these ingredients.

CASTING A SACRED CIRCLE

A circle creates a protective place in which to create magick. It makes a space that takes you out of the mundane world and into a protected, energized bubble, to cast spells. Here is one of many ways to cast a sacred circle to work your magick.

- Clear a space for your circle. Taking four candles, place one in the North of the circle, one in the East, one in the South and one in the West. Walking clockwise around the circle, light each candle in turn, sprinkling some salt as you walk from one candle to the next, to create a boundary for your circle.

- Facing North, point your finger or wand to the floor and say: 'Guardians of the North, element of earth, I bid you hail and welcome.' Now face East, keeping your finger or wand pointing to the floor, and say: 'Guardians of the East, element of air, I bid you hail and welcome.' Face South, keeping your finger or wand pointing to the floor, and say: 'Guardians of the South, element of fire, I bid you hail and welcome.' Face West, keeping your finger or wand pointing to the floor, and say: 'Guardians of the West, element of water, I bid you hail and welcome.'

- Face North again and point your finger or wand above your head. In a clockwise motion, cast your circle, starting above your head and bringing your finger or wand down to the right, then back up to the left to finish above your head again. You can now start your spell.

- When you have finished your spell, simply walk out of the circle to break it, effectively bringing its power to an end.

HOW TO MAKE MOON WATER

Moon water infuses a spell with an extra touch of magick. Use it in your rituals, add some to your ritual bath or drink some before casting a spell.

- Select a clean glass jar and fill it with water – spring water is ideal. Hold the jar and set positive intentions. If you intend to drink the moon water, cover the jar with a lid.

- Place the jar outside or on a windowsill where it can be exposed to the moonlight, preferably on the night of a full moon. Allow the moonlight to penetrate the water.

- Collect the water at dawn to capture the moon's energy. Store the moon water in the fridge for up to three days.

HARNESSING THE POWER OF A FULL MOON

Before starting a spell, use your hands to create a triangle by placing the tips of your index fingers together and placing your thumb tips together. Hold your hands up to the night sky and gaze at the moon through the triangle you have made. After a few moments, close your eyes, still seeing a vision of the moon. Bring the triangle down and place it up against your solar plexus, thus harnessing the moon's energy.

the SPELLS

MOONSTONE CRYSTAL SOUL HEALING

Cast this restorative spell on a full moon phase, whenever you feel you need to clear negative energy on a soul level. The moon has the ability to heal our souls, drawing out any negativity we have absorbed. It's not easy if you feel you have been wronged by a friend or are feeling generally depleted of positive energy. Life can be difficult if you don't feel whole. This spell will help to clear anxiety, depression and hurt, whether recent or from years ago.

MAGICKAL CORRESPONDENCES

- White candle in a holder
- Lighter
- Moonstone crystal

On a full moon, create a special space in your home, where the moon can shine on you if it's a clear night sky. If it's cloudy, visualize a full moon. Take a ritual shower to cleanse your energy beforehand. Sit quietly and contemplate, light the candle and hold the crystal next to your solar plexus. Imagine a silver light radiating from the crystal and surrounding you in a protective bubble. Whisper the following magickal words:

Moonstone crystal, on this full moon night,
Heal my soul, embrace the light.
Under the full moon's beams, pure and bright,
Restore my spirit, renewed and bright.
So mote it be.

Visualize the healing energy flowing from the moonstone and healing any emotional wounds. Envision it clearing negative energy in the moonlight. Take your time to absorb the healing essence.

Express gratitude to the moonstone and the moon above. Carry the crystal with you or place it under your pillow so that its healing vibrations continue to nurture your soul as you embrace a renewed sense of well-being.

2

ROSE QUARTZ HARMONY

Cast this nurturing spell on a Friday, on a waxing moon phase. Rose quartz crystals are associated with loving energy. They are often found in heart-shaped jewellery. This spell has been created to clear stress and promote healing and inner harmony.

MAGICKAL CORRESPONDENCES

- Pink candle in a holder
- Lighter
- Rose quartz crystal

Create a peaceful space in which you can unwind. Light the candle and hold the rose quartz crystal close to your heart, connecting with its loving energy. Take a deep breath and close your eyes, allowing any negative feelings to be released with each exhale. Visualize a gentle pink light surrounding you, filled with love and positivity. Feel the warmth of this energy being absorbed into every cell of your body, soothing away all your stress and promoting inner peace and harmony. Whisper the following magickal word:

Rose quartz crystal of love so true,
Fill my heart with kindness anew.
Banish all doubts and fears I wear,
With candle's gentle glow,
self-love I declare.
So mote it be.

Cast this spell whenever you feel the need to recharge your energy.

3
MOON MAGICK

Cast this calming spell on a new moon phase.

MAGICKAL CORRESPONDENCES

- Moonstone crystal

On a new moon, find a comfortable spot outdoors where you can observe the serenity of the moon. Hold your crystal next to your heart, close your eyes and take a few slow, deep breaths. Allow the softness of the air to caress your face as you connect with the serenity of the magickal moon. Visualize a silver thread extending from the moon to your heart. Feel a deep sense of calm as you connect with the moon's energy; feel uplifted and balanced. Say the following magickal words:

Beautiful moon, with your gentle light,
Bring harmony to my tired mind.
Banish worries and anxieties deep.
With your serenity, calmness I will keep.
So mote it be.

Visualize the moonlight surrounding you in a beautiful glowing silver bubble, replacing any negative thoughts or feelings with its soothing aura. Take a few more slow, deep breaths, inhaling the moon's peaceful energy, and exhale any tension that you may feel. Hold your crystal for a few moments before you go to bed and sleep with it under your pillow to connect with the moon's calm vibrations.

4
MAGICKAL WATER BOTTLE

You can cast this rejuvenating spell on any moon phase. Water is the essence of life and making a magickal water bottle is an essential part of self-care. This spell keeps you hydrated with each sip of water infused with positive and mystickal properties. The spell changes ordinary water into a magickal crystal elixir, promoting natural healing and cleansing your body, while adding the energy of enchanted crystals.

MAGICKAL CORRESPONDENCES

- Water bottle with a lid and a straw
- Spring water
- Rose quartz crystal
- Citrine crystal
- Clear quartz crystal
- White candle in a holder
- Lighter

Create an altar (see page 12). Wash the bottle and dry it. Place the spring water on your altar with the crystals next to it. Clear your mind and light the candle. Place your hands over the spring water. Whisper the following magickal words:

Water and crystals, an enchanted blend,
Energize and heal,
Intentions ascend.
With each sip nourishing my soul,
This spellbound water will make me whole.
So mote it be.

Place the crystals inside the bottle and pour the spring water over them. Snuff out the candle and bury the remaining wax near a lake, pond or stream.

Witchy Tip
Wash and dry crystals before using, and never use soft crystals as they can be toxic.

5
CANDLELIT SELF-CARE BATH

Cast this recharging spell on any day, on a waxing moon. This bath spell has been created to soothe the mind, body and soul using herbs, candles and crystals to create a relaxing and refreshing experience. In magick the element of water governs emotions, and it also cleanses and clears negative energy. Lavender is long known for its calming scent, chamomile for its relaxing properties and rose petals for self-love. Amethyst crystals enhance the spiritual connection. The combination of these elements recharges your energy and allows you to relax and focus on self-care.

MAGICKAL CORRESPONDENCES

- Purple candles in holders
- Lighter
- Lavender oil
- Rose petals
- Chamomile flowers
- Amethyst crystals

Set the scene. Dim the lights, play soft, relaxing music and pop your phone into silent mode to avoid any interruptions. Run the bath to the temperature that suits you, then light the candles. Add a few drops of lavender oil to the bath, sprinkle the rose petals and chamomile flowers over the water and add the crystals. Step into the bath and take a few slow deep breaths. Whisper the following magickal words:

> *This bath has now become a spell,*
> *A rippling sacred flow*
> *In the candlelight's flicker,*
> *A soft and gentle glow*
> *Warming water's embrace,*
> *A self-care ritual, a serene space.*

Visualize all negative energy flowing out of your body into the bathwater. Lie in the bath for as long as you feel comfortable then, when you pull the plug out, visualize the negative energy draining away from you and being replaced with light and crystal-clear energy. Snuff out the candles. Keep the crystals next to your bed and place the petals and any remaining wax from the candles beneath a rose bush.

6

GREEN SMOOTHIE DETOX

Cast this detoxing spell on any day, on a waxing moon. Drinking a green smoothie is a great way to cleanse the body and raise your energy levels. In the realm of spiritual wellness, a green detox smoothie spell uses the power of nutritious ingredients to cleanse the body and restore energy.

MAGICKAL CORRESPONDENCES

- Blender
- Spinach
- Kale
- Cucumber
- Fresh mint
- Coconut water
- Lemon juice
- Glass

In the blender, place a handful each of fresh spinach, for renewal, and kale, for strength. Add half a cucumber, for purification and hydration and a handful of invigorating mint leaves, for clarity and balance. Pour in a glass of coconut water, symbolizing purity, and a squeeze of lemon juice for its cleansing properties. Blend the ingredients together and pour the smoothie into the glass. Place your hands over the top and whisper the following magickal words:

Coconut water, a liquid so pure,
Lemon zest, a cleansing allure,
Spinach and kale, their powers combine,
Cucumber for purity, mint for charm.
A detox green spell, a healing balm.
So mote it be.

Sip the fusion and feel any toxins exit your body, leaving you feeling totally revitalized.

7

PERSONAL POWER

Cast this spell of empowerment on a waxing moon phase, on the Thursday night nearest to a full moon. Thursday is Jupiter's day, symbolizing power and expansion. This spell has been created to unlock the power that already resides within you and to expand your self awareness. Also, the energy of the tiger's eye will boost your confidence.

MAGICKAL CORRESPONDENCES

- White candle in a holder or tealight
- Lighter
- Tiger's eye crystal
- Paper
- Pen

Find a quiet place where you won't be disturbed. Light the white candle to create a calm and focused atmosphere. Take a moment to centre yourself and connect with the energy of the crystal – hold it in your hand and visualize a bright, golden light surrounding you. On a piece of paper, write down your wishes in terms of personal power and self-confidence. Be clear about your intentions. Fold the piece of paper three times towards you and hold it between your palms. Close your eyes and visualize the desired outcome as vividly as you possibly can. Place the folded paper under the crystal. Place your hands over the crystal, focusing on its energy merging with your wishes; absorb the energy, feeling your personal power growing stronger. Whisper the following magickal words:

> *By sun and moon, this spell is spun.*
> *My personal power has begun.*
> *Tiger's eye, a crystal bright,*
> *Ignite within a potent light.*
> *In shadows deep, where whispers fly,*
> *Rise up, let power rise high.*
> *So mote it be.*

When you feel you have absorbed all the energy from the crystal, snuff out the candle and bury it with the piece of paper under an oak tree. Keep the tiger's eye crystal close to you during the day and under your pillow at night.

8

REJUVENATE ME

Cast this energizing spell on a Sunday, on a waxing moon. It is a simple yet powerful way to rejuvenate your mind, body and spirit. Self-care is essential to nourish your soul and to uplift your spirit.

* * *

MAGICKAL CORRESPONDENCES

- Naturally scented candle
- Lighter
- Lavender or chamomile oil

Create a peaceful space where you can relax and be undisturbed for a while. Light the candle and place it in front of you. Take a few deep breaths, inhaling the tranquil aroma and exhaling any tension or stress you may have. Relax, close your eyes and visualize a warm, healing light surrounding your body from head to toe. When you feel you have connected to this positive and serene energy, rub a small amount of the essential oil into your wrists or temples. Gaze into the flame and say the following magickal words:

> *I call upon energies pure and bright,*
> *Candle flickers into the night.*
> *Oils of healing, potion to brew,*
> *A dash of essence, rebirth anew.*
> *So mote it be.*

Take your time to relax and enjoy this moment, respecting the love and care you are showing yourself. Allow the candle to burn right down. Bury any remaining wax under a rose bush. Repeat this spell whenever you feel stressed, drained or depleted of positive energy.

9
BANISH ANXIETY

Cast this powerful anti-anxiety spell on a dark moon phase. It has been crafted to create a sense of calmness and inner peace in your everyday life.

MAGICKAL CORRESPONDENCES

- Extra-virgin olive oil
- Lavender oil or dried lavender
- Small dish
- Small white candle in a holder
- Lighter
- Clear quartz crystal

Find a quiet space in which to cast this spell – a place where you can relax and be at ease without interruption. In the small dish, mix a drop of olive oil with a pinch of lavender or a drop of lavender oil and use it to anoint (rub) the sides of the candle, avoiding the wick. Take a few deep breaths to ground yourself, then light the candle. Hold the clear quartz crystal and visualize a bright glow coming from the flame and creating a protective bubble around you. Gaze into the flame and whisper the following magickal words:

*As this candlelight flickers a soft and gentle light,
I cast this spell into the night.*

Anxiety, I now release you.
Peace, I now welcome you.
Let calm be mine
With this enchanted rhyme.
So mote it be.

Visualize all thoughts of negativity disappearing from your mind and being replaced with a sense tranquillity. Leave the candle burning, allowing you to absorb its magickal energy. When you feel you are ready, snuff out the candle and bury any remaining wax with any leftover herbs in the woods, away from your home.

SELF-CARE LOVE JAR

Cast this uplifting spell on a Friday, on a waxing moon phase. This spell will enhance your well-being, allowing your spirit to soar. Pink candles, roses and rose quartz crystals have long been used in self-love magick. Lavender and hibiscus bring a calmness that soothes the spirit. Creating this spell in a jar combines all the loving energy, keeping it pure and strong.

MAGICKAL CORRESPONDENCES

- Pink candle in a holder
- Lighter
- Glass jar with a lid
- Hibiscus flowers
- Rose petals
- Lavender
- Ground cinnamon
- Rose quartz crystals

Light the candle, then place the flowers, petals, herbs and spices in the glass jar. Add the rose quartz crystals on top. Hold the jar and whisper the following magickal words:

*Under the crescent moon's tender glow,
A self-love spell jar, let its energies flow.
Candle of pink, so divine,*

*Dancing flame, let self-love shine.
So mote it be.*

Seal the lid of the jar – and with it your spell – with some wax, then snuff out the candle. Keep the jar in a special place in your home, holding it every morning for an extra boost of self-love. Bury the candle under a rose bush.

SWEET DREAMS

Cast this bedtime on spell on a Monday, on a waxing moon phase or any time you feel you need help with your dream pattern. We all need to have a good night's sleep to wake up feeling recharged and refreshed. This simple chamomile spell with allow you to have a good night's sleep and sweet dreams. Chamomile works wonders on relaxation and lavender releases all your stresses and worries.

MAGICKAL CORRESPONDENCES

- Purple candle in a holder
- Lighter
- Lavender flowers
- Chamomile flowers
- Small pouch

As you prepare for bedtime, light the candle on your dressing table or windowsill and then mix equal quantities of chamomile and lavender flowers. Visualize calming images and positive energy as you do so, and add them to your pouch. Hold the pouch and whisper the following magickal words:

*Beneath the moon's soft glow,
I release all worries and let them go.
With chamomile and lavender's calming embrace,
I drift into a sweet slumber space.
So mote it be.*

Snuff out the candle. Before sleeping, focus on your intention for sweet dreams, reciting a calming affirmation or a simple chant. Inhale the soothing scents of chamomile and lavender, allowing them to relax your mind. As you drift into slumber, let the combined energies of these herbs promote tranquillity and guide you to a restful night's sleep.

GODDESS VENUS INNER BEAUTY

Cast this spell of wish fulfilment on a Friday before a full moon. Friday is governed by the goddess Venus, who resides over love and beauty. Invoking her into this magickal spell creates a beautiful, uplifting boost to self-esteem and self-care. Create a serene space, play soft music, light a rose-scented candle. Roses attract love and self-love, jasmine attracts confidence and allure, and hibiscus attracts confidence and self-expression.

MAGICKAL CORRESPONDENCES

- Pink candle in a holder
- Lighter
- Bowl
- Rose quartz crystal
- Rose petals
- Jasmine flowers
- Hibiscus flowers
- Moon water (see page 14)
- Mirror

Centre yourself before starting: take a few deep breaths and focus on what it is you wish to achieve; visualize the end result. Light the candle. Place the rose quartz crystal in the bowl then sprinkle a few petals and flowers on top. Pour moon water over the flowers, until the bowl is more than half full. Place your hands, palms down, over the bowl, look at yourself in the mirror and whisper the following magickal words. Repeat them three times adding more passion each time.

Goddess Venus, I ask for your grace.
Within my beauty, let light embrace.
With these flowers' inner power,
My inner beauty blossoms like a flower.
So mote it be.

Pour the water under a rose bush or in a special place in your garden. Place the flowers on top and keep the rose quartz crystal near to you at all times.

13

PROTECTION SPELL

Cast this spell of protection on a Saturday, on a waning moon phase. Saturday is governed by the planet Saturn, which has incredible power when invoked into a protection spell. Black candles absorb negative energy and the black crystal increases this powerful spell's potency.

* * *

MAGICKAL CORRESPONDENCES

- Black candle
- Lighter
- Black tourmaline crystal

Create a quiet and comfortable space where you can focus without distractions. Light the candle and hold the black tourmaline crystal in your hands. Close your eyes. Take a few deep breaths and clear your mind. Visualize a protective bubble being formed around you, reflecting any negative energy away from you. Whisper the following magickal words:

*Saturn's energy, strong and true,
With this black tourmaline
Shield me from harm, protect and renew.
Negative energy, I now repel,
With black tourmaline,*

*All will be well.
So mote it be.*

Allow the candle to burn down and bury any remaining wax under a holly bush. Keep the black tourmaline crystal close to you or in a safe place to keep its protective energy going strong for you.

14

EMOTIONAL HEALING

Cast this healing spell on a Sunday, on a waxing moon phase. This spell has been created to heal inner wounds, allowing your spirit to dance and be free. The pink candle represents unconditional love and healing energy. Lavender allows the mind to relax, cinnamon brings warmth and comfort.

MAGICKAL CORRESPONDENCES

- Pestle and mortar
- Lavender flowers
- Rose petals
- Ground cinnamon
- Extra-virgin olive oil
- Pink candle in a holder
- Lighter
- Rose quartz crystal

Begin this spell by creating a quiet and comforting space in which you can fully connect with yourself and your emotions. Use the mortar and pestle to grind a few lavender flowers and rose petals and sprinkle in some cinnamon. Rub a little oil onto your candle and sprinkle the flower mix over the candle. Light the candle, allowing its gentle glow to envelop your aura, creating a serene and calm atmosphere. As you inhale the soothing aroma of lavender, allow your mind to quieten and release any negative emotions you may be carrying. Hold the rose quartz crystal in your hands, feeling its warm, loving energy resonating within you. Visualize a beautiful pink light encompassing your heart, filling it with love and self-acceptance. Allow this loving energy to clear away any pain or hurt, replacing it with love, tranquillity and peace. Then say the following magickal words:

> *Emotions be soothed, as this spell is cast,*
> *Healing my heart, healing me fast.*
> *With this candle, lavender, cinnamon, and rose,*
> *Peaceful serenity within me flows.*
> *So mote it be.*

Allow the candle to burn right down and bury any remaining wax with the herbs and flowers in a special place in your garden or in the woods. Keep the rose quartz crystal close to you, to keep that sparkling feeling of self-love for your emotional well-being.

ANTI-DEPRESSION SPELL

Cast this spell of banishment on a Sunday, on a waning moon phase.

MAGICKAL CORRESPONDENCES

- Tealight
- Lighter
- Glass jar with a lid
- Pink salt
- Cloves
- Lavender flowers
- Peel from an orange
- Peel from a lemon
- Clear quartz crystal
- Rose quartz crystal

Light the tealight in a quiet and calm space. Place the jar in front of you and add a pinch of pink salt to it. Crush a few cloves and sprinkle them over the salt, then take a handful of lavender flowers and sprinkle them over the cloves and salt. As you sprinkle them, focus on releasing any negative energy or feelings of depression. Once you've done that, take the orange and lemon peels and place them on top of the lavender. Close your eyes and inhale, allowing the scent of the citrus peels to lift your spirits, bringing you positive and happy thoughts.

Take the crystals in your hands, gaze into the flame and say the following magickal words:

> *In a bowl of pink salt, this spell I weave.*
> *Cloves of strength, my spirit retrieve.*
> *Lavender whispers tranquillity near,*
> *Clear away darkness, let hope reappear.*
> *Orange and lemon's zest, a burst of delight,*
> *Banish the gloom, protect me with your golden light.*
> *So mote it be.*

Snuff out the flame knowing that you have banished any darkness from your mind. Keep the spell jar in your bedroom, or any area where you spend a lot of your time, and keep the crystals close to you all the time. Whenever you feel a little down, light another tealight, take the lid off the jar and breathe in the relaxing scent. Allow the positive energy to encompass you, clearing away any negative thoughts you may have.

YOUR INNER GODDESS

*Cast this spell of invocation on a full moon.
It has been created to celebrate your own
inner goddess.*

MAGICKAL CORRESPONDENCES

- Jasmine oil
- Candlewood oil
- Red candle in a holder
- Lighter
- Rose petals
- Paper
- Pen
- Moonstone crystal

Create a peaceful space, take a few deep breaths and anoint your candle with a drop each of the two oils, avoiding the wick. Light the candle and sprinkle the rose petals around it. Reflect on the qualities you want to have – for example, kindness, inner beauty, charm. Visualize yourself already having these qualities. Write the qualities down on a piece of paper, using the present tense.

For example: 'I have inner beauty, I am confident.' Sign your name at the bottom. Fold the paper three times towards you and hold it in the palms of your hands with the moonstone crystal. Gaze into your candle flame and whisper the following magickal words:

> *Whispers of the universe, hear my plea.*
> *Awaken the goddess that resides within me.*
> *A blossoming rose, my inner flower,*
> *With every breath I draw your celestial power.*
> *So mote it be.*

Allow the candle to burn right down and bury any remaining wax and rose petals under a rose bush. Always keep the piece of paper under your pillow and the moonstone crystal close to you.

Witchy Tip
Always work in a clockwise (deosil) direction when you anoint a candle, as this will attract energy to you. Anointing a candle in an anti-clockwise (widdershins) direction will repel or push away energy from you.

YOUR INNER CHILD

Cast this spell of reconnection on a full moon. Embracing and healing your inner child creates a profound shift in your overall well-being, leading to increased self-awareness, better relationships with others and a sense of wholeness and inner peace. Rose quartz is for self-love and amethyst is for stress relief and protection. Lavender is good for lifting your mood and chamomile relaxes your mind.

MAGICKAL CORRESPONDENCES

- Scented candles
- Lighter
- Rose quartz crystal
- Amethyst crystal
- Lavender flowers
- Chamomile flowers
- Pouch

Find yourself a peaceful place and create a calm atmosphere. Light some scented candles and dim the lights. Put the crystals and flowers into the pouch. Sit in a comfortable chair or lie on a sofa or in bed. Close your eyes for a few moments to centre yourself, breathing in the scent of your pouch. When you feel centred, open your eyes and whisper the following magickal words:

*Heal the wounds the inner child may know.
With enchanted crystals, let their energy flow.
Gentle words, a lullaby from the past,
Inner child's healing, make peace at last.
So mote it be.*

Keep the pouch by your bed. Each night, inhale its healing scent and hold the crystals to absorb their extra nurturing power.

BANISH YOUR WORRIES

Cast this spell of banishment on a dark moon phase. The dark moon is one of the most powerful times to banish anything that no longer serves you well. Tea tree oil is a useful ingredient for clearing negative thoughts and jasmine is great for replacing worries with positive feelings. A black candle is the ideal tool to banish any kind of negativity.

MAGICKAL CORRESPONDENCES

- Small dish
- Extra-virgin olive oil
- Jasmine oil
- Tea tree oil
- Black candle
- Lighter

Create a quiet and comfortable space in your home where you will not be disturbed. In the small dish, mix a teaspoon of olive oil with a drop each of jasmine and tea tree oil. Use it to anoint the candle from its middle to the top, avoiding the wick, and then from the middle to the bottom. Visualize all your worries being absorbed by the candle as you do so. Light the candle. As it flickers, concentrate on your worries, visualizing them transferring to the candle's flame.

Sitting comfortably in front of the candle, take a few deep breaths, inhaling the calming scent of the tea tree and jasmine and exhaling all your worries. Visualize a protective golden bubble around you, protecting you from anxious thoughts, and envision a calm atmosphere enveloping you. Whisper the following magickal words:

> *With this black candle burning bright,*
> *Banish my worries into this dark moon night.*
> *So mote it be.*

Repeat the words three times, saying them with utmost passion. Allow the candle to burn right down and bury any remaining wax under a holly bush.

19
FEEL MORE POWERFUL

Cast this spell of empowerment on a Tuesday or Thursday, on a waxing moon. This spell has been created to tap into your inner strength. Working with either Mars (Tuesday) or Jupiter (Thursday) adds tremendous power to this spell.

MAGICKAL CORRESPONDENCES

- Fresh rosemary
- Red candle in a holder
- Paper
- Pen
- Cauldron or heatproof dish
- Lighter

Arrange a sprig of fresh rosemary, the candle, a piece of paper and the pen around the cauldron or heatproof dish. Light the candle, focusing on its flame. Take a deep breath to ground and centre yourself. Write the following magickal words on the piece of paper:

In this cauldron, power to be bound,
I cast this spell with words profound.
Light of the candle, mesmerizing glow,
Inner strength, let it flow.
So mote it be.

Hold the piece of paper and visualize yourself feeling powerful and strong. Infuse this energy into the paper, and when you feel ready, place it in the cauldron, sprinkling a little of the rosemary on top, and set it alight using the candle. To increase the intensity of the spell, say the words out loud, gazing at the paper burning in the cauldron. Allow the paper to turn to ashes and the candle to burn right down. Bury the ashes with any remaining candle wax under an oak tree and place the sprig of rosemary on top. Thank the universe for your newfound power.

PSYCHIC PROTECTION

Cast this spell of protection on a Saturday, on a waxing moon phase. Have you ever been in someone's company and felt drained afterwards? If so, this is the spell for you. Some people can naturally drain you of your energy, so it's important that you protect it. Working with Saturn's energy, with its protective rings of ice, will add extra potency to this spell.

MAGICKAL CORRESPONDENCES

- Sage smudge stick
- Lighter
- Cocktail stick
- Black candle
- Fresh rosemary
- Allspice
- Black tourmaline crystals

Light the smudge stick to cleanse the area in which you will be casting your spell. Create a calm space and sit in front of the candle. Use the cocktail stick to etch your initials inside a circle into the candle. Sprinkle some rosemary and allspice over the candle and arrange the black tourmaline crystals around it. Visualize a protective shield around you. Light the candle, gaze into the flame and whisper the following magickal words:

Saturn with your beautiful rings of ice,
This spell I cast with crystals and spice.
With herbs, candle and crystals combined,
Protection and strength
I shall find.
So mote it be.

Visualize a protection bubble around you and feel the power it has to deflect any negative energy. Snuff out the candle and bury any remaining wax under a holly bush. Keep the crystals in a safe place.

SELF-CONFIDENCE SPELL

*Start this confidence-boosting spell
on the night before a full moon. It has been created
to give your confidence a lift if you have experienced
a setback, and is cast over three nights.*

✦ ✦ ✦

MAGICKAL CORRESPONDENCES

- Bowl
- Dried basil
- Ground cinnamon
- Ground ginger
- 3 white candles in holders
- Lighter

Create a peaceful space in which to cast your spell. Set the scene with soft music and dim the lights. Make sure you will not be interrupted. Mix the herbs and spices in the bowl and sprinkle them over the three candles. Start feeling the energy building. Light the candles and feel the energy grow stronger as the flames flicker. Close your eyes and connect to your old self. Reclaim your energy, visualizing the powerful and positive energy all around you being absorbed into each and every part of your body. Snuff the candles out when they have burned down by one-third. Place the candles next to your bed while you sleep.

Repeat the exact same steps on the second and third nights, allowing the candles to burn down by one-third each time. Again, each night, after casting the spell, keep the candles next to your bed. When the spell is over, bury any remaining wax under a special tree and blow the leftover herbs to the wind.

UNCROSSING SPELL

*Cast this spell of banishment on a dark moon phase.
This spell has been created to remove obstacles
that stop you moving forward.*

MAGICKAL CORRESPONDENCES

- Sage smudge stick
- Lighter
- Heatproof dish
- Extra-virgin olive oil
- Sea salt
- Black candle in a holder
- Paper
- Pen
- White candle in a holder

Create a quiet space for your ritual. Make it comfortable and be sure that you are not going to be interrupted. Cleanse your space using the smudge stick. In the dish, mix a few drops of olive oil with a little salt and anoint the black candle, starting at the middle to the top then from the middle to the bottom. Turn the candle anti-clockwise as you do so and avoid getting oil on the wick. Light the black candle, concentrating on the obstacles you wish to remove. Visualize removing them from all areas of your life. Write them down on a small piece of paper, then light the paper from the flame of the candle and allow it to burn down in the heatproof dish. As it burns down, visualize all your obstacles turning into ash. Snuff out the black candle then light the white candle and whisper the following magickal words:

> *Guiding light, my path anew,*
> *Candles charged, a beacon true.*
> *I stand renewed now, unbound,*
> *A new way forward has been found.*
> *So mote it be.*

Allow the white candle to burn right down and bury any remaining wax along with the black candle in a forest or woods away from your home.

23

NEW BEGINNINGS

Cast this spell for a new start on a new moon, a time for leaving past challenges behind and creating a magickal journey. This spell promotes a fresh mindset and sense of well-being.
The Death tarot card represents saying goodbye to what no longer serves you and the re-birthing of a new you. This is a time to transform and welcome new beginnings as one door closes and another one opens. The natural scent of lemons will purify your space and leave a fresh and clean fragrance.

MAGICKAL CORRESPONDENCES

- Water spray bottle
- Lemon
- Water
- Cloth
- Glass vase
- Biodegradable silver glitter
- Tealight
- Death tarot card
- 3 white roses
- Lighter

Squeeze the juice of half a lemon into the water spray bottle and fill the rest with water. Spray and wipe your space with the cloth. Fill the vase with water and place it on a windowsill. Sprinkle a little glitter on the tealight and place it on the windowsill. Lay the Death tarot card and the white roses next to the tealight. Light the tealight and say the following magickal words:

> *Goodbye to the old as*
> *Destiny unfolds*
> *A new chapter for me.*
> *So mote it be.*

Allow the tealight to burn until it extinguishes itself and place the remaining wax in the bottom of the vase with an extra sprinkle of the silver glitter. Stand the three white roses in the vase. Nurture them by changing the water every day and cutting a tiny piece from the bottom of the stems. Place the tarot card next to the vase on the windowsill, knowing a new chapter has now begun. Enjoy your journey.

GODDESS BATH OIL

Cast this rejuvenating spell on a Friday, on a waxing moon phase. This goddess bath oil will help you unwind, leaving you feeling energized and rejuvenated. Each essential oil contains calming and soothing properties, and the peppermint leaves will clear your senses as you indulge in this magickal self-care ritual.

MAGICKAL CORRESPONDENCES

- Candles
- Lighter
- Small, clear dropper bottle
- Peppermint leaves
- Sweet almond carrier oil
- Lavender oil
- Chamomile oil
- Lemongrass oil
- Rose geranium oil
- Clear quartz crystal

Prepare the bath oil in advance: first, place two peppermint leaves in the bottom of the dropper bottle and fill the bottle with approximately 100 ml (3½ oz) of almond oil. Add two drops each of lavender, chamomile and lemongrass oil, and one drop of rose geranium oil. Take your time and create a serene ambience in your bathing space. Light candles and play soft soothing music to create a peaceful and tranquil setting. As you run the bath, add three drops of the bath oil to the water and slowly step into the bath while it is still running. Centre your thoughts, close your eyes and meditate to the sound of the music. Breathe in deeply the aromatic scent of the oils and say the following magickal words:

> *Beneath the stars,*
> *I embrace*
> *A tranquil ritual*
> *In my sacred space.*
> *Empowered, renewed,*
> *Intentions aligned.*
> *Awakening magick,*
> *Feeling divine.*
> *So mote it be.*

Take the clear quartz in your hand and relax, knowing that the power of the clear quartz will amplify your thoughts, wishes and desires. Now simply lie in the bath until you feel you are ready to step out.

Witchy Tip
It is important to patch test the bath oil on your skin before using it.

25
CLEAR MY SKIN

Cast this spell of banishment on any day, on a waning moon. Eliminate blemishes and acne with this powerful removal spell. Tea tree essential oil is known to kill bacteria and tame blemishes and inflammation of the skin. Using a black candle with tea tree oil is a powerful combination for a banishing spell.

MAGICKAL CORRESPONDENCES

- Small dish
- Extra-virgin olive oil
- Tea tree oil
- Black candle in a holder
- Lighter
- Hand mirror

In the small dish, mix a teaspoon of olive oil with two drops of tea tree oil, and use it to anoint your candle, turning it clockwise and avoiding the wick. Visualize yourself with radiant and clear skin. Light the candle and gaze into the flame. Hold the mirror in one hand, and looking at your reflection, slowly point to the areas on your face, highlighting areas you want the spell to work on to remove. Take your time as you do this. Keep gazing at the candle, visualizing the flame removing the areas that you touch. Say the following magickal words:

Magickal mirror in my hand,
I ask for skin as clear as crystal.
As I touch my face I now know
My skin is going to magickally glow.
So mote it be.

Take some deep breaths and allow the candle to burn down. Bury the remaining wax by a clear river or pond.

CLEANSE MY HOME

Cast this spell of banishment on a dark moon. Remove unwanted lingering energy in your home by cleansing your space to promote positive vibes. You can cleanse your space using bells, a singing bowl, by clapping or burning incense. Black tourmaline is a powerful and protective crystal that helps to absorb negative energy. It has a grounding effect that leaves you with a sense of calm.

MAGICKAL CORRESPONDENCES

- Sage incense and a holder
- Lighter
- Bells
- 4 black tourmaline crystals

Light the incense and walk slowly to each corner of the room in turn, moving in a clockwise direction and making a circle with the smoke. This allows every corner of the room to be cleansed. Place the incense in a holder. Cleanse the bells and each black tourmaline crystal by clapping over them. Place a crystal on the floor in each corner of the room. Take the bells and chime them in each corner. Whisper the following magickal words:

*As I cleanse the energy and set it free,
Tranquillity now resides.
So mote it be.*

Centre yourself for 10 minutes, after which the energy should feel lighter, pure and vibrant.

CLEANSING AURA SPRAY

Create this cleansing aura spray on a waxing moon phase. It is a moon mist spray that encourages a moment of reflection, promoting positivity and well-being and cleansing your energetic aura field. Charge and cleanse the amethyst crystal before using it by pouring spring water on it and leaving it out under a full moon.

MAGICKAL CORRESPONDENCES

- Measuring cup
- Distilled water
- Witch hazel
- Tea tree oil
- Rose geranium oil
- Lemongrass oil
- Lavender oil
- Amethyst crystal
- Large spray bottle

Pour 500 ml (1 pt) of distilled water into the measuring cup and add 250 ml (½ pt) of witch hazel. Add two drops of tea tree oil and one drop each of rose geranium, lemongrass and lavender oil. Place the amethyst crystal at the bottom of the spray bottle and pour the mixture on top. Softly whisper the following magickal words:

*Mystick mist a spray so fine,
All your energies now align.
With each gentle spray, all is well.
Essences twirl a vibrant spell.
So mote it be.*

Spray a gentle mist over your head and under your toes every morning and before going to bed to allow the gentle fragrances to work and cleanse your aura.

SIMMERING SELF-CARE SOUP

Create this nourishing soup on any moon phase. Grounding vegetables and herbs make a perfect concoction of flavour for warming you up on cold days. For a heartier soup, try adding a handful of pasta or lentils.

MAGICKAL CORRESPONDENCES

- Large saucepan
- Extra-virgin olive oil
- 1 onion
- 1 clove garlic
- 2 carrots
- 1 stick celery
- 1 handful green beans
- ¼ cabbage
- ½ leek
- 1 parsnip
- 1 white or sweet potato
- 500 ml (1 pt) vegetable stock
- Tomato paste
- Sprig of thyme
- Ground cinnamon
- Paprika
- Bay leaf
- Fresh coriander
- Bowl

Prepare, wash and chop the onion, garlic, carrots, celery, green beans, cabbage, leek, parsnip and potato. Heat one tablespoon of olive oil in the saucepan and add the onion and garlic. Add the carrot, celery, green beans, cabbage and leek, and sauté on a low heat, then add the parsnip and potato.

Add the vegetable stock to the pan and a squeeze of tomato paste. Bring to the boil and season with thyme, cinnamon, paprika and the bay leaf. Allow to simmer gently for 20 minutes, checking and stirring occasionally. As the soup simmers on a low heat, say the following magickal words:

> *A dash of mindfulness,*
> *A sprinkle of peace,*
> *A time to let all worries cease.*
> *For I am grounded and renewed*
> *As this magickal soup has brewed.*
> *So mote it be.*

When the soup has been brewed, remove the thyme and bay leaf, pour into a bowl and garnish with some sea salt and black pepper. Finally add a sprinkling of fresh, chopped coriander.

Create a relaxing ambiance and set your table with candles, flowers or herbs. Enjoy this magickal infused soup, being mindful you are nourishing your mind, body and soul.

GOLDEN HOUR MILK

Cast this spell any time you want a good night's sleep. This earthy and grounding milk is perfect at bedtime for sweet dreams. Set your intentions and calm your mind at this golden hour. Turmeric is known to be a healing spice and has been used in traditional medicine for centuries.

* ✷ *

MAGICKAL CORRESPONDENCES

- Mug
- Small saucepan
- Coconut or almond milk
- Ground turmeric
- Ground cinnamon
- Ground nutmeg
- Honey or maple syrup
- Vanilla extract
- Black pepper
- Sea salt

Heat a mugful of milk in a saucepan over a low heat. Add half a teaspoon each of turmeric, cinnamon and nutmeg, and gently bring to the boil. Simmer for a short while, then stir in a teaspoon of honey, half a teaspoon of vanilla extract, a pinch of black pepper and a sprinkle of sea salt. Whisper the following magickal words into the saucepan:

An elixir of enchantment nurtures my soul.
Golden milk's warmth makes me feel whole.
As I whisper under the moon's soft glow,
Magickal milk, your essence shall flow.
So mote it be.

Pour the milk into the mug. Take a sip of your milk as you snuggle under a cosy blanket and visualize yourself having the best night's sleep.

EMBRACE YOURSELF WITH HAPPINESS

Cast this self-love spell on a Sunday, on a waxing moon phase. Rose quartz is known as the crystal of love and brings peace and tranquillity.

MAGICKAL CORRESPONDENCES

- Pink tealights
- Lighter
- Pink bath salts
- Small bowl
- Red strawberries
- Sugar
- Rose quartz crystal

Take a relaxing bath before casting this spell. Place two pink tealights on the edge of the bath and add a handful of pink salts to the water to deeply detoxify and cleanse your body. The warmth of the pink is soothing and will bring a calm feeling of peace and harmony.

After your bath, prepare a bowl of juicy red strawberries and sprinkle some sugar on top. Sit for a moment and meditate with the rose quartz crystal, visualizing yourself full of happiness and self-love. Embrace the self-love within you and start to eat the strawberries. Eat slowly and mindfully.

Once you have eaten the strawberries, hold the rose quartz crystal and whisper the following magickal words:

Happiness flows through me,
As do love and positivity.
Within my heart I do believe
That all I need I shall receive.
So mote it be.

Sleep with the rose quartz crystal under your pillow to inspire pleasant dreams and the radiation of positive vibrations within.

HEALING MUFFINS

Cast this spell of well-being at noon on a full moon. Heal your spirit and awaken your senses as you warm your soul with the sweet scent of cinnamon and the aroma of lavender. Lavender and blueberries pair very well – the subtle taste of the lavender brings out the sweetness of the blueberries.

MAGICKAL CORRESPONDENCES

- Large bowl
- Wooden spoon
- Small bowl
- Muffin cases
- 100 g (3½ oz) unsalted butter
- Granulated sugar
- 2 eggs
- ½ tsp lavender essence
- 1 tsp vanilla extract
- 140 g (5 oz) natural yoghurt
- 2 tbsp buttermilk
- 250 g (9 oz) plain flour
- 2 tbsp baking powder
- 1 tbsp bicarbonate soda
- Blueberries

Topping:
- Brown sugar
- Ground cinnamon
- Sea salt

Heat the oven to 200°C (390°F). In the large bowl, blend the butter and sugar together until pale and fluffy, then beat in the eggs. Gently mix in the lavender essence and vanilla extract. Beat the mix some more, then add the yoghurt and buttermilk. Fold in the flour, baking powder and bicarbonate of soda and add a pinch of salt. Gently mix in the blueberries, then drop a tablespoon of the mixture into each muffin case. In the small bowl, combine the brown sugar with half a teaspoon each of cinnamon and sea salt. Sprinkle a little on each muffin. Bake for 25–30 minutes and whisper the following magickal words:

Self-care moments in this space of retreat,
As I nourish my soul, self-love is complete.
So mote it be.

Once the muffins have been baked, allow them to cool down. With each one that you eat, feel it healing you from the inside out.

COMFORTING BEDTIME CACAO

Make this magickal bedtime cacao on any day of the month. Cacao is one of the most abundant sources of magnesium. Known as the 'sleep mineral' this natural relaxant makes a perfect addition to a cosy bedtime ritual. This spell not only warms you inside and out, but also nourishes you, preparing your body for a restful night's sleep. Adding cinnamon gives greater depth of flavour and sea salt combines all the flavours together.

MAGICKAL CORRESPONDENCES

- Bowl
- Whisk
- Saucepan
- Mug
- Wooden spoon
- Oat milk
- Cacao
- Vanilla essence
- Ground cinnamon
- Maple syrup, to taste
- Sea salt
- Marshmallows

In the bowl, whisk together one mugful of milk with half a tablespoon of cacao, half a teaspoon of vanilla essence and a sprinkle of cinnamon. Transfer to the saucepan and warm over a low heat. Add some maple syrup, stirring in a clockwise direction, and pour into your mug. Sprinkle the cacao with some sea salt and top with marshmallows. Place your hands gently around the mug and whisper the following magickal words:

> *In each velvety sip, I find*
> *Cosy comfort,*
> *A peaceful mind.*
> *Inner peace echoes in harmony,*
> *Fulfilled and aligned.*
> *So mote it be.*

Dim the lights and relax as you slowly indulge your senses. As you drink your bedtime cacao, visualize being filled with positive vibrations.

33
SPARKLING SELF-CONFIDENCE

Cast this confidence-boosting spell on any day of the week, on a waxing moon phase, and release your inner goddess from within. The scent of orange will enhance and impact your mood and the uplifting golden tones of this spell will leave your aura dazzling. Sunstone is known as the stone of joy and will inspire strength and power.

MAGICKAL CORRESPONDENCES

- Incense stick
- Lighter
- Sunstone crystal
- Small dish
- Extra-virgin olive oil
- Orange oil
- Gold candle in a holder

Cleanse your space using incense before you begin and gently blow onto your crystal to activate its energy. In the small dish, mix a teaspoon of olive oil with two drops of orange oil. Anoint your candle, working in a clockwise direction and avoiding the wick. Light the candle, and holding the crystal close to your solar plexus, say the following magickal words:

Confidences flame like the rising sun,
A new chapter has now begun.
As I rise and chant loud and clear,
A confident and bold me will now appear.
So mote it be.

Meditate with your crystal for 10 minutes and visualize your new confidence growing. Now harness the power to push forward and be that new, confident you. Bury your candle and leave your crystal on top.

BUTTERFLY MEDITATION

Cast this healing spell on any day of the week, on a waxing moon phase. Heighten your senses and heal your vision. A beautiful butterfly is here to guide you to transform and heal your emotions. Burning eucalyptus oil in your ritual cleanses and purifies your space, leaving you in a state of pure and tranquil bliss.

MAGICKAL CORRESPONDENCES

- White tealight
- Lighter
- Eucalyptus oil

Create a peaceful sanctuary space, light the tealight and add two drops of eucalyptus oil. Lie quietly as you visualize a beautiful butterfly. Give the butterfly a name; the butterfly is your friend. As the butterfly flutters its wings, take a moment to kindly give all the things you want the butterfly to carry away with it. Meditate and spend time with your butterfly. Release all your burdens – your butterfly is here to carry them away with its glorious wings. When you feel ready to release, whisper the following magickal words:

*Butterfly's wings a ritual of release,
Shedding unwanted layers,
Finding inner peace.
Butterfly with your wings so light,
I say goodbye,
I now feel warm and light.
So mote it be.*

The butterfly hears your words and slowly flutters and drifts away into the sky, taking what you no longer need with it. Wish goodbye to the butterfly, with your thanks.

35

EMPOWERING SELF-LOVE

*Cast this spell on the Friday before a full moon.
It is time to enhance and nurture yourself with self-love
from within. Lemons are cleansing and bring positive
energy into a space, while lavender is calming and
promotes emotional healing. The soothing aroma of rose
and its petals will allow love to gently flow and blossom.*

MAGICKAL CORRESPONDENCES

- Incense stick
- Lighter
- Lemon
- Knife
- Small plate
- Extra-virgin olive oil
- Lavender oil
- Pink candle
- Rose petals

Set up an area where you are comfortable and will not be disturbed. Lightly cleanse the space with a little incense before you begin. Slice the bottom from the lemon and stand it on the plate. Now cut a cross shape in the top of the lemon. Mix half a teaspoon of olive oil with two drops of lavender oil and use this to anoint the candle, working in a clockwise direction. As you do this, relax and take deep breaths, visualizing a white light comforting and surrounding you. Stand the candle upright in the lemon and then light the flame. Slowly whisper the following magical words:

> *I am worthy, I am enough.*
> *I deeply nourish myself with self-love.*
> *So mote it be.*

Spend some time with the candle as it burns, meditating on the qualities you appreciate about yourself, and allowing this energy to absorb deeply within. Once the candle flame has burned out, bury the lemon in a safe, quiet space in the ground, by the roots of a tree, and sprinkle a handful of rose petals on top. Give thanks and blessings to the goddess of love, Aphrodite.

SEVEN CHAKRAS HEALING

Cast this spiritually healing spell on any day of the month. Using this spell will cleanse and encourage harmonious energy flow by clearing any negative energy and emotional blockages.

MAGICKAL CORRESPONDENCES

- Clear quartz crystal (crown)
- Amethyst crystal (third-eye)
- Blue lace agate crystal (throat)
- Green aventurine crystal (heart)
- Tiger's eye crystal (solar plexus)
- Citrine crystal (sacral)
- Red jasper crystal (root)
- Spring water

Cleanse the crystals in spring water. Find a peaceful place to lie and place each crystal on its corresponding chakra on your body. Whisper the following magickal words:

Crystals aligned, energies combined,
Chakras flow, harmony I find.
As I balance and align,
My energy feels so divine.
So mote it be.

Allow the energy to flow for 20 minutes as you embrace the energy and rejuvenate.

Chakras

Chakras are tiny energy points that centre along the spine from the pelvic area to the crown. Each of the seven main chakras is associated with a colour and affects certain aspects of our emotional and physical well-being.

- The silver crown chakra is located above the head and gives us sense of direction in life, guiding our highest state of spiritual awareness.

- The indigo third-eye chakra is located in the centre of the brow and guides our inner wisdom and intuition.

- The blue throat chakra symbolizes expression and communication.

- The green heart chakra is located in the chest area and symbolizes love and our connection with others.

- The yellow solar plexus chakra is below the ribs and symbolizes our determination, emotions and sense of self.

- The orange sacral chakra is below the belly button and symbolizes our creativity and passion within our self and life.

- The red root chakra is at the base of the spine and is the energy that grounds and balances us.

EMBRACE YOUR BEAUTY

Cast this beauty spell on a Friday before a full moon. Before you call upon Aphrodite, be sure to embrace your beauty with the clothes and make-up you will be wearing. Colours of Aphrodite are white, red and gold – choose to wear them for special occasions.

MAGICKAL CORRESPONDENCES

- White and pink rose petals
- White tealight
- Jasmine oil
- Lighter

Use the rose petals to create a small circle and place the tealight in the centre. Add two drops of jasmine oil. Light the candle and say the following magickal words:

*I call on you goddess Aphrodite
To shine your beauty on me.
Hair that shines, skin that glows,
Beautiful like you, now I am whole.
So mote it be.*

Allow the tealight to burn until it extinguishes, then bury the remaining wax in a rose bush. Lay the petals on top.

SELF-CARE SPELL FOR ARIES

Cast this empowering spell on a Tuesday, on a waxing moon phase. Ariens are naturally fiery, fierce and bold. This spell will enhance your physical and mental being.

MAGICKAL CORRESPONDENCES

- Red tealight
- Black pepper
- Lighter

Sprinkle a pinch of black pepper onto the tealight and light the wick. Ground yourself by gazing into the flame. Visualize a warmth running from your toes, through your body and up to your head. Say the following magickal words:

*Candle flame as your charge my soul,
And use your magick to make me whole.
Standing tall, bold and strong,
Ready to conquer what comes along.
So mote it be.*

Remember, you are the fuel you bring to the fire and the powerful ram that takes charge of all situations headfirst. You have the power.

39
INDULGENT BATH RITUAL FOR TAURUS

Cast this pampering spell on a Friday, on a waxing moon phase. A Taurean's determination is strength, but now is the time to unwind, relax and indulge your senses in this bath-time ritual. Take care of your physical and emotional needs by aligning your desire for stability and finding a sense of balance and positivity. Known for its calming properties, oat milk soothes and nourishes the skin. Have fluffy towels ready for after your bath and wrap yourself in a silk or satin robe.

MAGICKAL CORRESPONDENCES

- Oat milk
- Seashells
- Soft pink tealight
- Lighter
- Geranium oil

Begin with soft lighting and create a soothing ambience by playing some light music. Run a warm bath, adding one cup of oat milk to the water. Decorate your bath with seashells to create a serene atmosphere, symbolizing a soothing connection to the ocean. Light the tealight and add two drops of rose geranium oil to the tealight and one drop to the bath. Say the following magickal words:

*Magically I have the power
To create what I desire.
Strength and stability,
Pure bliss and luxury.
So mote it be.*

Relax and take time to recharge and pause your mind. Allow the tealight to burn until it extinguishes itself. As you leave the bath, hydrate, moisturize and get cosy. Take a few moments to reflect on your bath ritual experience. Sleep with the seashells beside you to infuse your soul with magick and energetically charge you as you sleep.

RELAXATION SPELL FOR GEMINI

*Cast this unwinding spell on a Wednesday, on a waxing moon phase. Creating a balance between mental stimulation and relaxation is crucial for a Gemini, allowing you to unwind and foster a sense of harmony while sustaining your vibrant energy and maintaining the relationships you have with those around you.
A Gemini's love for communication and interaction, and your constant flow of thoughts and ideas can sometimes lead to exhaustion and burnout. Using two candles represents the duality of Gemini and the colour, light blue, symbolizes Gemini's air element.*

MAGICKAL CORRESPONDENCES

- Paper
- Pen
- Small cauldron
- 2 light blue tealights
- Lavender oil
- Lighter

Use a piece of paper and the pen to spend some time journaling. Express your thoughts, your wishes and your feelings. Explore the shadowy aspects of any challenges, obstacles or fears you are working through. As you do this, you will transform these shadows to strengths.

Place the tealights in the middle of the cauldron and add two drops of lavender oil to each. Fold your journaling paper in half and then in half again. Hold the paper to the flame of a tealight and allow it to burn down. Then say the following magickal words:

> *Time to breathe.*
> *Time to unwind.*
> *Time to revitalize my mind.*
> *Breathe in tranquillity, let my worries go.*
> *Exhale gently, let serenity flow.*
> *So mote it be.*

Allow the flame to burn down on both tealights then bury them in an open area. This will allow the magickal energies to circulate and carry your intentions into the air, amplifying them.

Witchy Tip
If possible, keep a window slightly open to connect to the element of air, and visualize the wind carrying away any unwanted obstacles.

NOURISHING SPELL FOR CANCER

Cast this hydrating water spell on a Monday, on a waxing moon phase. Nourish your mind and soothe your emotions as you replenish and hydrate your senses while infusing and invigorating your soul. Cancer is a water sign and Cancerians are highly sensitive to their own emotions and the energy and emotions that surround them. Shells represent the flow of life and are associated with the goddess Aphrodite. Their connection to the ocean will enhance healing and spiritual well-being.

MAGICKAL CORRESPONDENCES

- Clear quartz crystal
- Jug
- Water
- Fresh peppermint
- Lemon
- Wooden spoon
- Shell
- Cup

Create a safe space in your home. Before starting, charge your crystal: hold it in your hands and visualize the outcome of the spell. Take a jug of water, add some fresh mint leaves and squeeze in some lemon juice. Stir in a clockwise motion, visualizing your intention, then place the charged quartz crystal in the centre. Place the shell in front of the jug, then say the following magickal words:

> *Magick water cleanse my soul.*
> *Magick water make me whole.*
> *With waves of energies, enchantments start.*
> *I have peace, clarity and strength in my heart.*
> *So mote it be.*

Pour some of the hydrating water into a cup and take a few sips. As you drink the water, do so knowing you are absorbing energy from the goddess Aphrodite with her healing powers. Drink as much of the water as you desire and then bury the crystal by a river or lake to enhance the connection between the crystal and the element of water. Visualize your crystal taking root and growing just like a seed as it sprouts and stands tall. Keep the shell close by on a windowsill.

SELF-CARE SPELL FOR LEO

Cast this sparkling strength spell on a Sunday, on a waxing moon phase. Leos love to take pride in themselves and should make this a time to reset. A self-care ritual is essential for Leos to recharge and maintain their inner strength, ensuring they feel valued, and honouring their own needs and confidence. Enhance this strength spell with a tiger's eye crystal and the Strength tarot card, which reflects courage and reminds you of your own inner strength.

MAGICKAL CORRESPONDENCES

- Sage incense
- Lighter
- Tiger's eye crystal
- Yellow tealight
- Biodegradable gold glitter
- Strength tarot card

Cleanse your space and the tiger's eye crystal using the incense. Take the tealight and lightly sprinkle gold glitter over the top. Light the wick. Place the Strength tarot card next to the tealight and put the tiger's eye crystal on top. Visualize a luminous golden light starting from the crown of your head and progressing down, infusing every part of your body and filling you with a sense of strength and warmth. With each breath, gently let this light illuminate your thoughts. Slowly take your time as you meditate and visualize these thoughts and feelings. Whisper the following magickal words:

> *I take this time to reflect.*
> *This time, I take to connect.*
> *To build my strength, and like the sun,*
> *Shine light and radiance for everyone.*
> *So mote it be.*

Allow the tealight to burn and keep the tiger's eye crystal in a sacred space or in natural sunlight to recharge and cleanse its energy.

NURTURING SPELL FOR VIRGO

Cast this nurturing spell on a Wednesday, on waxing moon phase. Virgo strives for perfection and is always taking on responsibilities, but now is the time to take a pause and relax. A little self-care allows a Virgo to connect to their emotional side and nurture their well-being, allowing them to recharge and maintain their emotional balance. Green is the colour for balance and growth – it aligns with Virgo's earthy and practical nature.

MAGICKAL CORRESPONDENCES

- Paper
- Pen
- Soil
- Small cauldron
- Green tealight
- Tea tree oil
- Lighter

Create a quiet, organized space and play some relaxing music. Take a piece of paper and write down exactly what it is you truly want for yourself. Take your time. Sprinkle a small handful of soil into the cauldron and place the tealight on top. Add two drops of tea tree oil to the tealight and light the wick. Fold the piece of paper in half and in half again, then allow the paper to burn in the cauldron. Say the following magickal words:

> *And as I take this moment to spare,*
> *Grounded and centred,*
> *Indulging in self-care.*
> *Tea tree scents and stars so bright,*
> *I welcome new energy*
> *With this flame so bright.*
> *So mote it be.*

Allow the flame to burn down, then take the cauldron and bury the candle, soil and ashes into the ground.

HARMONIZING SPELL FOR LIBRA

Cast this balancing spell on a Friday, on a waxing moon phase. Libra is governed by Venus the planet of beauty and love. The two pink tealights represent Libra's scales – they support the need for balance and harmony. The lavender infuses the space with peace and calm.

MAGICKAL CORRESPONDENCES

- Sage smudge stick
- Lighter
- 2 pink tealights
- Lavender oil
- Mirror
- Rose quartz crystal

Cleanse your space using the sage smudge stick before you begin and play sweet soothing music. Take some deep breaths to uplift your inner calm. Add one drop of lavender oil to each tealight and light them both. Sit in front of the mirror and reflect on areas of your life that need insight. Empower your thoughts by holding the rose quartz close to your heart and feel its calming energy radiating love. Whisper the following magickal words:

*Balance and harmony flows through me
As the soft wind blows.
So mote it be.*

Take time to meditate on your thoughts as the tealights burn down. Carry the charged rose quartz crystal with you at all times.

EMPOWERING SPELL FOR SCORPIO

Cast this spell of empowerment on a Tuesday, on waxing moon phase. Transform your soul and empower your mystical spirit within. Scorpios are known for their passion and deep intensity and frequently experience mental exhaustion. Self-care for a Scorpio allows them to nurture their emotional well-being and recharge. Scorpio is the ruler of the Death tarot card, which symbolizes endings, new beginnings and powerful transformation. Obsidian holds energies of grounding and protection to help align a scorpio's intensity and depth.

MAGICKAL CORRESPONDENCES

- Frankincense incense
- Lighter
- Obsidian crystal
- Patchouli oil
- Black tealight
- Death tarot card

Cleanse your space and the obsidian crystal thoroughly using the incense. Add two drops of patchouli oil to the tealight and light the wick. Place the crystal on top of the tarot card next to the candle. Whisper the following magickal words:

In shadows deep on this velvety night,
A dark flame burns, oh so bright.
Strengthened I am to the depths of my soul,
I lead the way, I have control.
So mote it be.

Gaze deeply into the flame and visualize your power. Place your hand on top of the tarot card and crystal, charging your energy and taking deep breaths. Allow the tealight to burn until the flame fades. Keep the crystal close to you. You now hold the power.

BATH RITUAL FOR SAGITTARIUS

Cast this vibrant and uplifting spell on a Thursday, on a waxing moon. Sagittarius possesses a spiritual and adventurous nature that can sometimes lead to burnout. Self-care is essential for this fire sign, providing stability and helping Sagittarius to navigate their cosmic path with grace and ease.

MAGICKAL CORRESPONDENCES

- Small Tibetan singing bowl
- Citrus-fragranced bath bubbles
- Orange rose petals
- Orange oil
- Orange tealight
- Lighter

Play some soft, uplifting music to create a relaxing ambience. Use the Tibetan singing bowl to cleanse both yourself and your space, removing any stagnant energy. After you feel cleansed, run your bath, adding the bubbles, and gently swirling the water in a clockwise motion, then sprinkle some orange rose petals in the bath. Add two drops of orange oil to the tealight and light the wick. Relax and rejuvenate for a short while in the calm waters of your bath and inhale the scents of the uplifting aromas. Visualize yourself as the Sagittarian archer shooting for the stars, take some time and meditate as you dance under the night sky. Take some deep breaths, then gently whisper the following magickal words:

> *Sagittarius let self-care begin.*
> *Nourish my spirit,*
> *Feel the fire within.*
> *As the flame flickers and starts to dance,*
> *My vibrational energy is beautifully enhanced.*
> *So mote it be.*

Gaze into the flame and imagine the flame is burning deeply within you and igniting your energy – this is your flame. Allow the candle to burn down and leave the bath when you feel ready to. With the tealight flame blown out, chime three times on the Tibetan bowl, holding it close to your heart. Bury the remaining candlewax in your garden or a plant pot.

47

GROUNDING SPELL FOR CAPRICORN

Cast this grounding spell on a Saturday, on waxing moon phase. Self-care is vital for the hardworking, dedicated and ambitious Capricorn, and provides the necessary balance between professional life and personal well-being. The uplifting nature of this spell ensures a Capricorn will feel rested and energized and can harmoniously pursue their ambitions. Garnet is Capricorn's empowering and grounding birthstone; it enhances strength and success. Rosemary brings in the earthy energy to boost mental clarity, healing and stability.

MAGICKAL CORRESPONDENCES

- Sandalwood incense
- Lighter
- Garnet crystal
- Rosemary
- Brown tealight

Use the sandalwood incense to cleanse your space and the garnet crystal before you start your spell. Sprinkle some rosemary over the tealight and light the wick. Hold the crystal in your right hand as you meditate and ground yourself, then whisper the following magickal words:

In a serenity of stillness,
Where we pause and take time,
A Capricorn finds balance,
Under the stars sparkling chime.
And as we take a deep breath,
And ground so deep,
In this beautiful haven,
A self-care retreat.
So mote it be.

Envision your feet being the roots of a tree and that you are standing tall and strong. The tree's branches are your arms and your hair as you sway happily from side to side. Take deep breaths to amplify your energy as you connect with the earthy nature of this spell, before returning to a balanced state of bliss. Blow this energy into the crystal in your right hand. When you are done, be sure always to keep your garnet by your side.

48
ENERGY SPELL FOR AQUARIUS

Cast this recharging spell on a Saturday, on a waxing moon phase. Aquarians are highly intellectual and independent. This spell will heighten your intuition, strengthening inner wisdom and encouraging self-confidence.

MAGICKAL CORRESPONDENCES

- Purple tealight
- Peppermint oil
- Lighter

Add two drops of peppermint oil to the tealight and light the wick. Gaze into the flame and take a few deep breaths to inhale the peppermint aroma. Visualize the flame's cleansing energy spreading balance and harmony. Whisper the following magickal words:

As I nurture my soul, and calm my mind,
Pause and breathe, give myself time.
I breathe in serenity and breathe out peace.
This is the time that I release.
So mote it be.

Meditate and take this time to recharge your mind as the candle slowly burns down.

SELF-CARE SPELL FOR PISCES

Cast this spell of self-reflection on a Monday, on a waxing moon phase. Self-care is essential for the mystickal and intuitive Pisces to maintain a sense of stability calm and clarity in their lives. Spending time in self-reflection will enable you to embrace the strength, power and positive creativity that lies within. Being a sign of empathy, Pisces can often absorb emotions from their surroundings without realizing it, so self-reflection is crucial. Take time to recharge your emotional well-being.

MAGICKAL CORRESPONDENCES

- Sage smudge stick
- Lighter
- Large bowl of hot water
- Lavender oil

Set up a quiet, tranquil space and light the smudge stick to cleanse yourself and your area before you begin. Gaze into the calming depths of the bowl of hot steamy water, envisioning a harmonious flow of emotions. Add two drops of lavender oil, inhaling the scent of the vapour as it rises into the air. Meditate on any intuitive insights or emotions you wish to release or enhance. Take time to reflect as you gaze into the water, taking deep breaths, and whisper the following magickal words:

*Healing water, reflect my soul.
Heal my aura,
Let my inner magick grow.
Self-love blossoms, a mystickal view.
The magick within me has now come true.*

Run a bath, then pour in the bowl of water. Climb in and relax deeply, connecting to the magickal and mystickal energies of your bath.

CLEAR YOUR MIND

Cast this spell on any day of the month. To activate your smoky quartz crystals, bury them in the earth for 12–24 hours before casting your spell. When you are feeling stuck and need to make a decision, this spell will bring the best out in you and guide you into making the right choice. 'Scrying' means to see and to discover, and it involves gazing into a reflective surface to connect to its energy and see visions. Smoky quartz crystals enhance your mood and will light your path, leading the way.

MAGICKAL CORRESPONDENCES

- 3 smoky quartz crystals
- Glass bowl of water
- Wand or stick

Hold the crystals in your dominant hand. Calm your mind and meditate on what it is you need guidance with. Take a few moments and then place the crystals into the bowl of water. Say the following magickal words:

*As above and so below,
Now I know which way to go.
Universe, you have guided me
And now the path is clear to see.
So mote it be.*

Take the wand and point it into the bowl of water creating a ripple effect. Take a deep breath and look into the bowl, scrying deeply. The guidance you are seeking will be shown as a clear vision.

spell
NOTES

SPELL NOTES

Many witches find it helpful to make notes of their spell-casting, and I recommend recording the details while they are fresh in your mind. It's a useful method to hone your craft by noting the intentions, thoughts, feelings and effects that arise during the process.

Here are a few ideas for details to write down:

- Date/time
- Moon phase
- Weather
- Name of spell and page number
- Intention of the spell
- How you felt before, during and after casting the spell
- Any other notes about what happened around the casting of the spell

The following pages are your sacred space to record your rituals for reflection.

_____

_____

_____

_____

_____

_____

SPELL NOTES

SPELL NOTES

SPELL NOTES

SPELL NOTES

SPELL NOTES

SPELL NOTES

SPELL NOTES

SPELL NOTES

INDEX
RESOURCES
ACKNOWLEDGEMENTS

INDEX

acne 64
affirmations 37
allspice 54
altar 12, 22
amethyst crystals 24–5, 48–9, 68, 86
anxiety 16, 20, 32–3, 50–1
Aphrodite 85, 88, 94–5
Aquarius energy spell 108
Aries self-care spell 89
aura, cleansing spray 68–9
aventurine crystals 86

banishment spells 11
    anti-depression 44–5
    home cleansing 66–7
    skin clearing 64–5
    uncrossing spell 58–9
    worries 50–1
basil 56
baths
    candlelit self-care bath 24–5
    oil 62–3
    Pisces self-care spell 110
    Sagittarius 104–5
    Taurus 90–1
beauty embracing 88
bedtime cacao 78–9
blueberry and lavender muffins 76–7
butterfly meditation 82–3

calming spells
    anxiety banishment 32–3
    candlelit self-care bath 24–5
    goddess bath oil 62–3
    love jar 34–5
    moon magick 20–1
    sweet dreams 36–7
Cancer nourishing spell 94–5
candles 9–10, 12–13
    anointing 32, 46–7, 50, 58, 64, 80, 84
    anxiety banishment 32–3
    empowering self-love 84–5
    feel more powerful 52–3
    Gemini relaxation spell 92–3
    inner goddess 46–7
    love jar 34–5
    protection spell 40–1
    psychic protection 54–5
    rejuvenation 30–1
    self-care bath 24–5
    self-confidence spell 56–7
    skin clearing 64–5
    sparkling self-confidence 80–1
    uncrossing spell 58–9
    see also tealights
candlewood oil 46–7
Capricorn grounding spell 106–7
chakras, seven chakras healing 86–7
chamomile
    candlelit self-care bath 24–5
    goddess bath oil 62
    inner child 48
    rejuvenation 30
    sweet dreams 36–7
cinnamon
    bedtime cacao 78
    blueberry and lavender muffins 76–7
    emotional healing 42–3
    golden hour milk 72
    love jar 34
    self-confidence spell 56
citrine crystals 22–3, 86
cleansing 9, 12, 16, 60–1
    aura spray 68–9
    candlelit self-care bath 24–5
    green smoothie detox 26
    home 66–7
    see also baths; incense
cloves 44–5
coconut milk 72–3
coconut water 26–7
cucumber 26–7

dark moon 32, 50, 58, 66
Death tarot card 60–1, 102–3
depression 16, 44–5
detoxing spells 26–7

emotional healing 42–3
empowerment
    Aries 89
    feel more powerful 52–3
    personal power 28–9
    Scorpio 102–3
    self-love 84–5
energizing spells 30–1, 62–3, 106–7, 108
energy ball 9
eucalyptus oil 82

Fridays
    beauty embracing 88
    empowering self-love 84
    goddess bath oil 62
    goddess Venus inner beauty 38
    Libra harmonizing spell 100
    love jar 34
    rose quartz harmony 18
    Taurus indulgent bath 90
full moon 14
    blueberry and lavender muffins 76
    inner child 48
    inner goddess 46
    self-confidence spell 56
    soul healing 16

garnet crystals 106–7
Gemini relaxation spell 92–3
ginger 56

goddess bath oil 62-3
golden hour milk 72-3
green smoothie detox 26-7
grounding spells 66-7, 102, 106-7

happiness embrace 74-5
harmonizing spells 100-1
healing spells
    blueberry and lavender muffins 76-7
    butterfly meditation 82-3
    emotional 42-3
    moonstone crystals 16-17
    rose quartz harmony 18-19
    seven chakras 86-7
    water bottle 22-3
hibiscus 34, 38-9
hydrating spells 94-5

incense 66, 80, 84, 96
inner child 48-9
inner goddess 46-7

jasmine 38-9, 46-7, 50-1
jasper crystals 86

kale 26-7

lace agate crystals 86
lavender
    anti-depression spell 44-5
    anxiety banishment 32
    and blueberry muffins 76-7
    candlelit self-care bath 24
    cleansing aura spray 68
    emotional healing 42-3
    empowering self-love 84
    Gemini relaxation spell 92-3
    goddess bath oil 62
    inner child 48
    Libra harmonizing spell 100
    love jar 34
    Pisces self-care spell 109
    rejuvenation 30
    sweet dreams 36-7
lemongrass 62, 68
lemons 12, 26-7, 44-5, 60-1, 84-5, 94
Leo self-care spell 96-7
Libra harmonizing spell 100-1
love jar 34-5

meditation 82-3, 108, 109
mind clearing 111-12
mint 26-7, 62, 94, 108
Mondays
    Cancer nourishing spell 94
    Pisces self-care spell 109
sweet dreams 36
    moon magick 20-1
moon phases 11
    see also full; new ; waning ; waxing
moon water 14, 38-9

moonstone crystals 16-17, 20-1, 46-7
muffins, blueberry and lavender 76-7

new beginnings 60-1
new moon
    moon magick 20
    new beginnings 60-1
nurturing spells, Virgo 98-9
nutmeg 72

oat milk 78, 90
obsidian crystals 102-3
orange 44-5, 80, 104

patchouli oil 102
peppermint 12, 94, 108
personal power 28-9
Pisces self-care spell 109-10
protection spell 40-1
psychic protection 54-5

quartz crystals
    anti-depression spell 44-5
    anxiety banishment 32
    Cancer nourishing spell 94-5
    goddess bath oil 62-3
    seven chakras healing 86
    water bottle 22-3

rejuvenation 30-1, 86
relaxation
    candlelit self-care bath 24-5
    Gemini spell 92-3
    sweet dreams 36-7
    Taurus indulgent bath 90-1
rose geranium oil 62, 68, 90
rose petals
    beauty embracing 88
    candlelit self-care bath 24-5
    emotional healing 42-3
    empowering self-love 84-5
    inner goddess 46-7
    love jar 34
    Venus inner beauty 38-9
rose quartz crystals
    anti-depression spell 44-5
    candlelit self-care bath 24-5
    emotional healing 42-3
    happiness embrace 74-5
    harmony 18-19
    inner child 48-9
    Libra harmonizing spell 100-1
    love jar 34
    Venus inner beauty 38-9
    water bottle 22-3
rosemary
    Capricorn grounding spell 106
    feel more powerful 52-3
    psychic protection 54
roses, new beginnings 60-1

sacred circle 13
sage
    incense 66, 96
    smudge sticks 54, 58, 100, 109
Sagittarius bath ritual 104–5
Saturdays
    Aquarius energy spell 108
    Capricorn grounding spell 106
    protection spell 40
    psychic protection 54
Scorpio empowering spell 102–3
scrying 111–12
self-confidence 28–9, 56–7, 80–1
self-love 84–5
self-reflection spells, Pisces 109–10
showers 16
skin clearing 64–5
sleep
    bedtime cacao 78–9
    golden hour milk 72–3
    sweet dreams 36–7
smoky quartz crystals 111–12
smudge sticks 54, 58, 100, 109
soul healing 16–17
soup 70–1
spinach 26–7
strawberries 74–5
Strength tarot card 96
stress
    rejuvenation 30–1
    rose quartz harmony 18–19
    sweet dreams 36–7
Sundays
    anti-depression spell 44
    emotional healing 42
    happiness embrace 74
    Leo self-care spell 96
    rejuvenation 30
sunstone crystals 80–1

tarot cards 60–1, 96, 102–3
Taurus indulgent bath 90–1
tea tree oil 50–1, 64, 68, 98
tealights
    Aquarius energy spell 108
    Aries self-care spell 89
    beauty embracing 88
    Capricorn grounding spell 106–7
    Gemini relaxation spell 93
    happiness embrace 74–5
    Leo self-care spell 96–7
    Libra harmonizing spell 100–1
    new beginnings 60–1
    Sagittarius bath ritual 104–5
    Scorpio empowering spell 102–3
    Virgo nurturing spell 98–9
Thursdays
    feel more powerful 52
    personal power 28
    Sagittarius bath ritual 104
tiger's eye crystals 28–9, 86, 96–7

tourmaline crystals 40–1, 54–5, 66
Tuesdays
    Aries self-care spell 89
    feel more powerful 52
    Scorpio empowering spell 102
turmeric 72

uncrossing spell 58–9

Venus inner beauty 38–9
Virgo nurturing spell 98–9
visualization 8, 9
    anxiety banishment 32–3
    butterfly meditation 82
    Cancer nourishing spell 94–5
    candle self-care bath 25
    emotional healing 43
    Leo self-care spell 96–7
    moon magick 20
    personal power 28–9
    protection spell 40
    psychic protection 55
    rejuvenation 30
    Sagittarius bath ritual 105
    skin clearing 64
    sweet dreams 36
    uncrossing spell 58–9
    worry banishment 50–1

waning moon 11, 40, 44, 64
water bottle 22–3
waxing moon 11
    Aquarius energy spell 108
    Aries self-care spell 89
    butterfly meditation 82
    candlelit self-care bath 24
    Capricorn grounding spell 106
    cleansing aura spray 68
    emotional healing 42
    feel more powerful 52
    Gemini relaxation spell 92
    goddess bath oil 62
    green smoothie detox 26
    happiness embrace 74
    Libra harmonizing spell 100
    love jar 34
    personal power 28–9
    Pisces self-care spell 109
    psychic protection 54
    rejuvenation 30
    rose quartz harmony 18
    Sagittarius bath ritual 104
    Scorpio empowering spell 102
    sparkling self-confidence 80
    sweet dreams 36
    Taurus indulgent bath 90
    Virgo nurturing spell 98
Wednesdays
    Gemini relaxation spell 92
    Virgo nurturing spell 98

RESOURCES

Starchild
7 High Street
Glastonbury
Somerset
BA6 9DP
www.starchild.co.uk
For herbs, oils, incense and candles

The Goddess and Green Man
17 High Street
Glastonbury
Somerset
BA6 9DP
www.goddessandgreenman.co.uk
For moon calendars, moon and planetary aspect diaries, candle holders and altar tools

The Crystal Healer
Suite F1, Unit 1,
The Verulam Estate
224 London Road
St Albans
Hertfordshire
AL1 1JB
www.thecrystalhealer.co.uk
For crystals that owner Philip Permutt sources himself from all around the world

ABOUT THE AUTHOR

Dee Johnson is a third-degree Wiccan High Priestess and expert spell-crafter. She has been teaching Witchcraft and Wicca for many years, helping others who are drawn to this ancient craft.

@themodern.witch
www.themodernwitch.co.uk

ACKNOWLEDGEMENTS

Thank you to Christopher Falconer, now in spirit, for his knowledge and for inviting me to join the Ashridge Coven. Also to my then coven sisters Christine and Linda and to my then coven brother Paul. They all gave me a tremendous amount of knowledge and time and we shared many meetings in Wendover and had such magickal and mystickal times. I feel blessed to have known them as part of my witch world. In more recent times, thank you to all my coven friends; we have shared so many magickal times.

I believe what is meant for you will never pass you by.